GODFIDENCE

To Confide in God
To have Confidence in God
To share one's existence with God

By
Laurence R. Smith

Cover Art: By Daniel DeLouise

First Printing 1990

ISBN: 0-914544-77-2

Published by:
Living Flame Press/325 Rabro Drive/Hauppauge, N.Y. 11788

Printed at Mark IV Press, Hauppauge, N.Y.

TABLE OF CONTENTS

"Laurence Smith has provided us with a refreshing opportunity through Holy Scripture to re-discover the spiritual journey without adornment.

In clear and dynamic fashion we experience wonderful opportunities for the uplifting of the human spirit."

The Right Reverend David E. Johnson, D.D.

The Episcopal Diocese of Massachusetts

INTRODUCTION

Living in the world is a task we all have been given. It is not an easy one.

How we go about this business of life is crucial to our well-being as well as that of our neighbors and the world. Those who seek to make sense out of living, to understand its joys and sufferings, come to face the reality of God, the creator and preserver of life.

Christians come to know God in a very special way: as a God of love and forgiveness who wants us to act the same. To be able to do this requires maturity—spiritual, emotional and, at times, intellectual.

Becoming mature is the result of a process of growth. Spiritual maturity involves the gaining of wisdom, which requires a person to have confidence in God. I call this Godfidence, and it is what this book is about. Godfidence is a collection of reflections that are discussions with God about life. They are conversations about becoming mature.

We are living at a time in which events are moving with such speed and complexity that spiritual maturity is more important than ever. The world needs mature Christians. God wants mature Christians.

PART ONE

Beginning Awareness

There is evil in the world and when people entertain it or are apathetic about it, it leads to suffering. God wants us to realize this, to recognize what is evil and what is good. He stays near us, shares the suffering with us and encourages us to work our way through it.

Preface
Cooperation With God

In the beginning God created the world,
and it was good . . .

. . . But it is people who create life on earth.

What will our creation be?

I
BEGINNING A DIALOGUE WITH GOD

There comes a time when we begin to question what is happening around us and in our own lives. We find ourselves inclined to seek God; to begin talking and, hopefully, listening for answers.

1. No Evil

You Have Heard It Said:

Hear No Evil

See No Evil

Speak No Evil

But What I Tell You Is:

Hear All Evil

See All Evil

Do No Evil

2. God Suffers People

God created people
In love
To love.

People,
Made in God's image—
Love—
Should love:
God
Themselves
Others.

Love
Is beauty
And truth.
Love is good.
Love is life.

We, like God,
Have a will.

6

God's will is to love,
Even though it hurts.
Our will may be not to love,
Even though it hurts.

We suffer.
God suffers.

Not to love is not to live.
The choice is mine.
The choice is yours.
The choice is ours.

God did not make us as slaves.
He made us free—
To choose
Love and life
Or to choose
Decay and death.

God calls us
To love;
Not as a king,
Demanding obedience from subjects;
We are called to love
Because love is perfect
Freedom.

We are free to choose perfection.
To choose it is to suffer in growth.
We can ask for help to grow.
We can help others to grow.
We can love God.
We can love ourselves.
We can love our neighbor.

People suffer people.

God suffers humanity

Because the end is worth it.
A vital, vibrant, freely giving,
Loving people
Will survive
And live with God;
Not in slavery without a will
But in freedom with a perfect will—
Love.

What will you choose?

3. Can You "No" Your Way to Happiness?

We say that God created us
And that God is perfect.
So unless God made a mistake,
Why are people so imperfect?

Or should we assume that we—
Struggling with our freedom to be ourselves
And our need to be obedient to you—
Make a perfect mess of things?

The answer is in defining perfection.

God created us with perfect freedom.
Not as a perfect machine.
Not as a perfect robot.
Not as a programmable slave.

But as a being capable of perfection:

8

Perfect freedom,
Perfect love.

Jesus showed us how.
Christ gives us the help
Through the Spirit
From the Father:
We are to be perfect,
As our God is perfect.

It is not an impossible dream.
It is not an order.
It is God's offer to us.
It is God's hope for us.

We have been sent
Many helpers:
Women and men
Who by their lives
Have become known to us
As prophets and saints.

God even went beyond this
Sending Jesus Christ
Beloved Son,
To show us the way,
To be our Savior.

God thereby leads us to discover
Who we are,
Where we can go,
What we can become:

Heirs
To everlasting life,

To everlastng love,
If we say yes
To walking with Jesus.

It is hard to say yes
And follow.

But
Does saying no make you happy?

4. The Hitchhikers

I was a long way from home, Lord.
Almost 500 miles.
We were on our way home from vacation—
The children, my wife, and I.
We were in another country.
It was early in the morning.
I was driving fast—60 mph—
Along the two-lane highway.

Then up ahead I saw a couple of hitchhikers.
Of course, I had no intention of picking them up,
Or even slowing down.
Hitchhikers can be dangerous.
So dangerous that we have laws against hitchhiking.
They frequently rob or harm
The good samaritans who pick them up.

I'm closer now. I can see they're not well dressed.
Well, that's typical
Of this generation of people
Who want a free ride!

Closer.
I'm surprised.

They're not young people; a middle-aged man

10

In a cowboy hat with his thumb out.
A couple of steps back is a woman,
Also middle-aged.
Her head's bowed.
She's not very pretty.
He's not very handsome.

Whoosh!
My eye takes it all in as I roar by.

It's all over in a few seconds
Moving at nearly 90 feet per second, the entire scene—
    recognition/passing—took but two, maybe three
    seconds.

Now they're behind me. They're in the past.
With every passing second they're 90 feet farther away.
In twenty-seconds, they're out of sight.

But not out of mind.

My mind replays the passing, seeing their faces;
The humbled posture of the woman;
The simple act of the man standing by the road
Asking for help—
Not proud, not arrogant, just there.

These people didn't look harmful; just needy.
It would have been a little cramped in the car
But we could have taken them in for awhile

As I think about it all over again, time goes by.
One minute, two minutes . . . they are two miles back
    now.
I struggle with going back.
But I don't.

Yet the scene haunts me.

11

More time goes by.
And I'm farther away.
Maybe someone else picked them up.
I'm too far away to go back now.

And I don't go back.

But I feel bad about it. Funny . . .

I never felt this way about passing hitchhikers before.
It was just something about these two people.

Was it you, Lord?
Did I pass you by?

I think maybe I did.
I think I didn't help when you asked.
I too, denied you.

Maybe—if I hadn't been in such a rush
I would have had time. Time to love.
It's funny—this idea of your being beside the road
Asking for help.
It never dawned on me before
But some passages from the Bible come to mind
From this experience.

After your resurrection,
Mary didn't recognize you
And thought you were the gardener.
Cleopas, on the road to Emmaus,
Didn't recognize you.
He and his companion had to insist
That you stay with them.
They had to allow you in
Before they knew you.

Peter and the others didn't recognize you
On the shore as they fished.

You told them to cast their nets
And John knew it was you
Only after they had done so.

Yet they acted.
And by using time rightly
They gained time—
Time for what was really important
And fulfilling.
The time they spent
In this encounter
Made them happy.
They were, thereby,
Blessed.

Lord, so often I seek but do not find.
I look but do not see.

Lord, teach me to love.
Help me to take time;
To slow down.

Now, Lord, another thought comes to mind,
And It frightens me:
"Lord, when did we see you
Hungry or thirsty,
A stranger,
Naked,
Or sick,
Or in prison,
And did not take care of you?"

Lord, have I passed you by today?

II
BEGINNING TO SEE
WORK AND SYSTEMS

As we grow, we perceive ourselves as living within a larger system than our individual selves. We realize the necessity of work; that we need goods and services in order to survive, and that we need to participate, to the extent we are able, in the provision of goods and services.

5. Death Wish?

For Christ is like a single body with its many limbs and organs, which many as they are, together make up one body. A body is not one single organ but many. If one organ suffers, they all suffer together. If one flourishes, they all rejoice together. Now you are Christ's body, and each of you a limb or organ of it.
(*1 Cor 12:12, 14, 26, 27*)

We, the people,
Are the body of Christ

And we are called to be a holy people.
We are promised help,
And also forgiveness for our failures.

We are promised so very much—
Eternal life and glory with God.
Yet so few accept Christ's call
With singleness of mind.
We generally do not take our spiritual nature seriously.

But then I think that most of us
Do not take our physical side very seriously either.
We all know that we should eat only nourishing foods
In proper quantities,
That we should not smoke or drink too much alcohol,
And that we should get a proper amount of regular
    exercise.

Yet we tend to overeat,
Eat junk food,
Smoke too much,
Drink too much
And exercise too little (or too much).
People literally kill themselves in this manner.

16

We have this beautiful earth to live on
And yet we devastate it in so many ways.
We foul the air.
We foul the water.
We foul the land.
In this manner we literally kill ourselves,
And our descendants, too.

We kill ourselves in many other ways:
With guns, automobiles, bombs, knives, and drugs.
We kill with malice.
We kill by accident.
We kill with indifference.
We even kill for peace.

Throughout all this we suffer;
And we complain about suffering
Then some say God is dead.
Others ask, God, "Why?"

I think God looks back on us and asks, "Why?"
God says,
I've given you everything you need to live
In love and peace and beauty and prosperity.
I offer you life and you pursue death.
I've given you prophets and Jesus to show you the way.
I've even given you a book on how to do it;
Yet so few read it or heed it.

Many of you wish for something better.
You wish for me to step in with power
To stop the oppression, pain and suffering.

And when I do not,
You turn and say that I'm dead.
Well, wishing is not enough.

17

You must seek to love.
With that mind-set I will help you.
I have told you this.
I have shown you this.
I would not have said it if it were not true.
Seek to love and you shall find love . . . and life.
Will you choose life
And work at loving in order to gain it?

6. Money and Labor

Mt 20:1-16: Laborers In The Vineyard. (The story of a
group of laborers who worked in a vineyard. Some
worked all day, some only an hour, yet all were given
the same wage; and the last were paid first.)

I read this story, Lord,
And it seems unjust
The way the workers were treated.

Why should people who work less
Be paid as much as those who work more?

And it seems cruel to insist that those
Who worked the shortest time be paid first,
In front of those who worked all day.
It's as if you wanted to taunt them.

It is only natural that those who worked all day
Would complain that they should get more pay
Than those who worked only one hour.

It seems harsh and unjust that you brusquely say
They have no basis for complaint,
Since they had agreed to the stated wage.

They feel aggrieved.
And mistreated.

18

They deserved more.
That's only natural.
Isn't it?

The justice, my child, was clear
When the workers agreed
To work for the wage offered.

It is not unjust for me to offer
To pay what I wish with my own wealth.

But you are missing the important point.
I wanted to show you that work is what is important.
I wanted to show you that unemployment is not good,
And that all people who seek work can and should be
    employed.

People need the fruit of each other's labor.
That is what is important.

Money is not that important.
I know you need money
But it is to exchange the fruit of your labor
For the fruit of someone else's labor.
And you need money to share with those in need.

Those who worked less than the full time
Did so not because they were unwilling to work
But because they were not hired.
They were there, ready to work
And thankful for the chance to work
And earn a living wage for the day.

The important point
Is that there is work to be done
In helping to create a loving world,
And that there can be enough money
To pay all who work a living wage.

Money is not real. Work is.

7. Human Suffering and Economic System

Love your neighbor
The Lord tells us.
But it is so hard to love.

We make it hard.
We create a system
To help us live better.
We called it The Economy!

It has helped us to do so very much;
So much that is good.

But it is indifferent
And lets us be selfish.

The Economy does not value love.
It values production
And consumption
And money.

We created The Economy to serve us.
But now we serve The Economy.

If people hurt The Economy
They must be corrected
Or discarded.

We suffer.
God suffers.

Lord, can we overcome this
And use the economy to serve all people better?

III

BEGINNING TO SEE OUR IMPACT ON OTHERS

As we live our lives, God tests us. In the testing we learn what we are like and begin to see what we want to be like.

8. What Seed Will You Sow?

The Kingdom of God is like this. A man scatters seed on the land; he goes to bed at night and gets up in the morning, and the seed sprouts and grows—how, he does not know. The ground produces a crop by itself, first the blade, then the ear, then full grown corn in the ear. (*Mk 4:26-28*)

The seed may fall on good soil,
On rocky soil, or among the thorns.
I know about this sowing of seed,
And that we need to be the right kind of soil
To bear the fruit of your seed, your word.

But, as I read this passage, Lord, the perception forms
  in my mind
That each one of us constantly casts seed upon the
  soil,
Wherever we go, whatever we do, whatever we say;
That each of us fails to sow your seed
Wherever we do not go; whenever we do not do, when-
  ever we do not say.

It seems, Lord, that you share with us the ability to create;
That the seeds we scatter create life on earth.

I look at the beauty you have created, Lord.
I look at the examples you have set for us.
I look at the teachings you have given us.

Then I look at the world we have created
For ourselves and our children and our grandchildren.
I look at the world we are creating.
And I ask, with a growing sense of apprehension,
What seed are we sowing?

I look around and see too much poverty and hunger,
Violence and killing, intolerance and fear,
Arrogance and selfishness, pollution and greed,
Sickness and blindness.

Lord, the seed for all this comes from us, doesn't it?

Yes, it does.
When my word is well rooted in you, and you grow,
The seed that you, in turn, produce and scatter
Is good seed.

That good seed—no matter where it falls—cannot produce bad fruit.

It may not grow but it is good seed and nothing bad
   can come from it.
Only good can come from it.

The thorns are not from my seed.
I'm glad you have come to see that.

As you say, you are always casting seed upon the soil.
You have the freedom and choice
To sow seeds of painful thorns
Or seeds of nourishing fruit.
The good seed—my word—is free.

My goal for you is simple but hard.
Sow love and we will grow a Garden of Eden.

I know this is simple to say and yet it is hard to do.
But I have not and never will
Leave you to do it alone.

I have sent you many helpers.
I have sent you my Son.
He is with you even now.
He knocks.

Will you open?
Will you cast good seed upon the earth?
Will you spread my word?

9. Snakes and Stones and Loaves and Fish

Is there a man among you who will offer his son a stone
when he asks for bread, or a snake when he asks for a
fish?
(*Mt 7:9-10*)

When Jesus asked that question
Nearly 2,000 years ago,
His own answer was that none would do so.

As bad as people were in that day,
They would not treat their child so badly.

But I think that some of us today do give our children a
   stone
When they ask for bread.
And expose our children to a snake
When they ask for a fish.

Most people do not treat their children
With malice and forethought
But rather in ignorance or indifference.

Consider a stone.
It is hard.
People can be injured or even killed with it.
It cannot be eaten. A stone is totally lacking in
   nourishment.
Fruit or vegetables cannot grow on it.

In sum, a stone is cold, hard, unyielding and
   unnourishing.

So when we give our children a cold, hard, unyielding
    world to live in,
We do indeed give them a stone,
When they are asking for bread.

Bread,
In Jesus' day,
Was a staple of life—
Whole grain, able to nourish.

Bread was broken and shared with others.

If we are to give bread and not a stone,
We must give what is good,
And not that which is empty of nourishment and
    harmful.

What about a fish and a snake?
How do we give our children a snake when they ask for
    a fish?

A snake is generally unseen.
Many people never see a snake, except in pictures, TV,
    or a zoo.
A snake is quiet. It is quick.
It can be poisonous and deadly.

It sometimes waits quietly for one to come near
Or it can suddenly appear
And strike.
This serpent
Is our environment.
What makes it dangerous
Are the poisons we make and throw around
Where our children can innocently stumble upon
    them.

We are poisoning our land, air, and water.
We poison our minds with prejudice, hate, and
   selfishness.
We poison our bodies with drugs and alcohol.

At times we let it happen
Through indifference, lack of knowledge, fear,
Or feeling helpless.

Even our economic system has become like a hidden
   viper
Waiting to strike some unsuspecting wayfarer
That disturbs it.

All of these examples are conditions
Not of nature or of God
But of humanity.

God calls us to change it.

We can
Make changes
In life . . .

Through an awareness of the world around us,
Study of God's word,
Prayer for others and with others,
Helping others as God leads us,
Increasing in goodness,
Returning to God:
For Life.

Is there one among you who will offer his son a stone
when he asks for bread, or a snake when he asks for a
fish?

What are you giving to others?

26

10. Sift You Like Wheat

Simon, Simon, take heed: Satan has been given leave to
sift all of you like wheat; but for you I have prayed that
your faith may not fail; and when you have come to
yourself, you must lend strength to your brothers.
(*Lk 22:31-32*)

You say so much, Lord,
In this single sentence.

We are shown that those whom you choose to bring
    close to you,
Who want to follow you and to share in your work,
Must face hard things.

It is so easy for us to think sentimentally
About you and the Father, and about love.
We think of falling
In love, if lucky;
Then basking in its warm glow,
As on a carefree sunny day.

But with these words of yours to Peter, Lord,
You show us that trials on our path to life cannot be
    taken from us;
That we will face difficult situations
Which can separate us from you—
Situations that seem too painful for us to face.

Yet we are not alone.
Your prayer intercedes for us.
Your prayer offers us hope.

I thank you that you pray for us,
As you did for Peter,
That our faith may not fail;

That although deflected from the path by fear and
    suffering,
We will turn again to you.

But, Lord, your prayer tells me that this is not enough.
Returning—being born again—is not an end.
We must,
Having turned again,
Help those around us.

Lord,
Will you strengthen our faith
That we may stay with you
And know when and how to strengthen our neighbors?

PART TWO

Looking to Grow

The Bible is replete with calls to seek wisdom and admonitions that the fear of God is the beginning of wisdom; for example, Proverbs 8 and James 3:17-18. We also find that God's commandments and guidance are intended for our own well-being.

As we study the Bible, develop a prayer life, and view the world in concert with God, these things become clearer. Living them may not be easier but it is possible to try.

The reflections in Part Two, Looking to Grow, help us to expand our understanding of the world and our part in it.

Preface
Growth in Christian Virtue

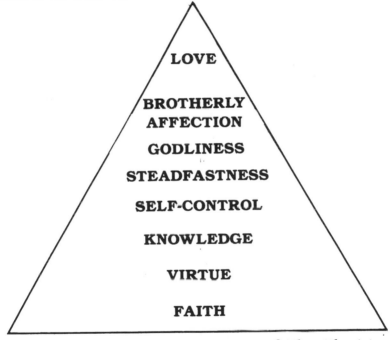

LOVE

BROTHERLY
AFFECTION

GODLINESS

STEADFASTNESS

SELF-CONTROL

KNOWLEDGE

VIRTUE

FAITH

Make every effort to supplement your faith with virtue,
and virtue with knowledge, and knowledge with self-
control, and self-control with steadfastness, and steadfastness with godliness, and godliness with brotherly affection, and brotherly affection with love.
(*2P 1:5b-11*)

IV
WORKING AT COMMUNICATION WITH GOD

A peaceful life may be something we have a right to, but it does not come free or without work. There is a price, whether we like it or not. We soon discover that our in-action, as well as action, is a cause that affects ourselves and others.

11. Does God Pray?

Prayer.
We hear a lot about it.
Jesus prayed.
He rose early to pray.
He stayed up late to pray.
Jesus tells us to pray.

His prayers were to our God who sent him:
Prayers for others,
Prayers for strength,
Prayers for power to love,
Prayers to do God's will.

We pray too.
We pray for love.
We pray for self,
Success, health,
And for others, too.

But is it all one-sided?
Do all prayers go one way?
From us to God?

What about God?
Does he just listen and answer?

No!
God does so much more than that.
God actively seeks us out.

In the beginning, Genesis,
God made a place for us
to live in.
At the end, Revelation,
God makes a place for us
To live in.

In between,
God reaches out to us
To become one,
With the creator,
Who answered Moses' question
As to who was speaking to him
By saying,
"I am."

The prayer of God
Is not simply pious words.
God's word
Is action.
It is life.

Think about all of the "Gods"
The mind of humankind has conjured up.
Then consider the one God of Israel
And Christendom:
A God who would love us,
Care about us, send people to teach us,
Even though we kill them,
And then decide to come personally,
To become, incredibly, a part of humanity,
In Jesus,
With a free choice to bring his humanity
Into perfection with God,
Accepting the humility of rejection,
The suffering of ignorance and arrogance,
The pain of false accusation and crucifixion,
In order to enable us to become the Body of Christ,
Heirs to the Kingdom of God.

We now have a connection with God
That will never be broken by him.

It is a connection of blood.
We are family.
The denial can come only from us.

God's desire is that we desire to accept the closeness
Of the Holy Spirit,
Living in a manner that is advancing toward purity
And holiness.

God desires this more than we do.

Perhaps we can look at God,
In our everyday lives,
As a coach
Who calls many to the tryouts;
And all who try out,
Giving it their best,
Make the team.

Only with this team,
There is no question of being good enough.
We all are good enough.
It is only a question of our desire
To love and be loved.

There is constant help available,
Among the coaching staff—
Father, Son and Holy Spirit.

There is ongoing prayer—
They talk to each other—
About us, for us,
And with us.

So it's up to you.
What is your prayer?
Do you want to be on God's team?

I hope so.
The other one is hell!

12. Strive with God

L 13:6-9: Parable Of A Fig Tree. For three years the fig tree bore no fruit and the owner told the vineyard keeper to cut it down. The vineyard keeper liked the tree, however, and asked for another year—to give him time to work on it and fertilize it. If it still did not bear fruit, it would then be cut down to make room for a fruit bearing tree. The owner agreed to give the keeper more time as he asked.

G 32:24-30: Jacob wrestles with God and when Jacob doesn't give up, God says, "Your name shall no longer be Jacob, but Israel; for you have striven with God and with man and have prevailed."

Life is a struggle, of many kinds.
We struggle with and against ourselves, others and
   God.

As hard as we work someone always seems to come
   along and complain—
As the vineyard owner did—about the one thing that
   isn't "right".
The fig tree was pretty and it gave welcome shade from
   the hot sun.
But that wasn't good enough for the owner—it had to
   bear fruit, too.

Jacob labored for twenty years, seemingly without
   complaint against God.

He had engaged in deceit with his family in order to be
   "number one",

And he in turn was a victim of deceit.
Yet he persevered,
Winning favor with God and forgiveness from his
  brother.

As I look at these two stories, Lord,
I am pulled in three directions.
One, a part that gets weaker as the years go by,
Is toward laziness.
You expect too much work, too much struggle,
Too much self-discipline.

Yet, I am also pulled in the direction of striving.
I like to work, to achieve, to compete, to accomplish
  things.
I feel good when the people I work with achieve.
And, like the vineyard owner,
I want to eliminate anything that does not bear fruit.

But even here, I can easily strive for my will, against
  yours,
As well as strive to know and do your will.

I can also sympathize with the manager
Who didn't mind the fig tree not bearing fruit—
That the cool shade it provided was valuable enough.

Thy will be done!

That's the hard part, I guess.
I mean, whose will is to be done?
My will . . . someone else's . . . or yours?

Or maybe we can take turns?
Doesn't that sound like a good compromise?

No?

Why does it always have to be your will?

You gave me a free will. Why can't I be free to use it?
How can it be a free will if you're telling me I have to do
  yours?

My will is life.
My will creates happiness.
That is also my will for you.
I am giving you a taste of life
And the freedom to learn about it,
Experiment with it, understand it;
To see the good and the bad,
The right and the wrong.

What I hope you will see is that life according to my
  will,
Because it is perfect,
Is good for everyone and is the only way for all to be
  happy.
Anything other than this is not good, it is evil.

If you will strive with me
You will know this.
Bearing fruit will be a natural outcome
Of your life,
Not an extra burden.

And knowing this you will see my will,
Not as an obstacle
To your will and your freedom,
But as a guide to your becoming . . .
Being born again into a new and unending life of joy
With no tears and pain.

Will you have faith
To strive with and for me
And my will?

V
SEEING EVIL

We all like to complain about evil and some declare God dead when the results of the evil and wicked are brought to light. Evil, however, is something that has to be dealt with by us, with God's help. We complain about trying to be good and do the right things when those who don't seem to follow God prosper while we struggle. We may be tempted to turn away from God and chase after the world to get our share; or to simply give up and withdraw from the world.

13. The Price of Peace

It is said, Lord, that love and truth will triumph
    over evil
And lead to a life of justice and peace.

Some believe.
Some disbelieve.
Others question how it can be achieved.

The Bible seems to show Jesus
Unwilling to fight for himself and his people.
His disciples questioned his tactics.
He was supposed to be the Messiah, the Savior,
Yet he made no defense to avoid crucifixion.

The worldly leaders,
Using typical violence,
Made an example of Jesus,
So others would succumb
To their worldly rule
And not challenge it.

Jesus let himself become their example
Only to turn the tables on them,
Showing the falseness of their ways.
He overcame the violence of the world
By losing his life in order to gain it.

A paradox?

God has shown us the end of the story.
The Bible shows us that there is war,
Between God and Satan, good and evil,
And that we are engulfed in this cosmic conflict.
We experience hate, cruelty, indifference.

Jesus defends humanity against sin,

Fighting the powers of evil,
Using the spiritual armor of God,
Proving that a life dedicated to God
Will not be crushed out.

The Bible tells us that Christ will gather his angels
To mount a final assault on Satan and his followers.
After that, Christ will raise his people
As God raised Jesus after the crucifixion.
He will create a new world—
Of everlasting peace.

Thus, the word of God is shown to be true:
Truth and justice will triumph.

But we live now, in this present age.
What about the peace we hear so much about?
When does this come?

This peace is an inner peace,
Rather than a peaceful life.

To gain peace you follow Christ,
Becoming examples, as he was;
Unafraid of bringing into the light of day
The evil desires and actions
Of people in church, government,
Business and society,
So that they may change and not harm people.

It may require offering life and freedom
against a violent and cruel foe.
It may require "turning the other cheek."
It takes prayer, study, and a Christian community
To understand more fully.
It takes commitment to Christ
To live the way.

This is, of course, the price.
A price involves something given up
In the course of obtaining another gain.

The price you pay
Is to incur a loss of evil
In the course of gaining God;
Or a loss of God
In the course of gaining evil.
There is no third option.

You have nothing to spend but your life.
To buy into God's world you have to give up evil.
To buy into the world of evil you give up God.

Let us pray to God the Father and to Jesus
For help to give up what is evil,
To have the wisdom and strength to do God's will,
And obtain the really good life.

14. Satan Versus Humanity

Satan,
The Tempter,
Works to tempt us
Away from God.

Why do Satan
And his fallen angels
Work so hard to draw us away?

Why are so many led astray,
Into so much suffering?

The Bible tells of Satan's fall from God
And of many angels being cast down with him.
Isaiah speaks of Satan wanting to have a throne
Higher than God's.

Satan rebels against God.
But why does he pick on us?

The Bible tells us about people, angels, God and Christ,
Satan and his disciples,
Heaven and earth,
Life and death.

God made people for a while lower than the angels.
But he also made us to be chidren of God.

Why, we do not know.

But we are heirs
With Christ
If we believe
And follow him.

Satan would not accept this.
Satan would not accept God's
Creation of humanity—a creation
That would put people higher than him.

Envy and pride
Welled up inside and overcame him;
And also many angels
Who followed Satan.

Their unrepentance left God no choice
But to cast them out.
Satan hates people because God loves them.
So Satan makes war
While people are weak and earthbound.

Satan got people to sin too,
And God had to deal with that sin:
Death came to be.

Jesus
Christ
Sacrificed himself
For humanity.
Jesus became human
And died for our sins.
We are saved!

Satan would not have us believe this.
And makes war to keep us from recognizing
And claiming our kinship to God,
In Christ.

That war is won!
Jesus won the war by resisting temptation,
Suffering a human death,
And being raised by God
In triumph over mortal cares.

Satan still does battle, he does not give in to God,
Even though he has no chance of winning.
Satan is unrepentant.

Will we,
Who follow Christ,
Be a priesthood of all believers
So that those who know him not
May learn the Gospel of redemption
And of life eternal?

15. Prosperity of the Evil

But I had nearly lost confidence; my faith was almost
gone because I was jealous of the proud when I saw that
things go well for the wicked. They laugh at other people and speak of evil things; they are proud and make
plans to oppress others.

I tried to think this problem through, but it was too difficult for me until I went into your Temple. Then I understood what will happen to the wicked. But as for me, how wonderful to be near God, to find protection with the Lord God and to proclaim all that he has done! (*Psalm 73:2,3,8,16,17,28*)

Lord, as I consider the evil that I see in the world
I can feel as the psalmist does
And speak to you in his words,
As though they were my own.
And yet it is not enough. I am still troubled.

If I were a mere observer of life,
It would be a comfort to see what becomes of the
     wicked.
It is nice to know that good will win.

But it bothers me to think of the millions
Who suffer and die
At the hands of the wicked
Or the neglect of the apathetic.
It is of little solace to be told that the wicked will pay—
     someday!

What about the victim?
What about the innocent people who suffer injustice
     and pain?
Are they like laboratory animals,
Part of some cold and inhuman experiment:
Where some are born in places of hardship—
Where poverty and disease are widespread;
And some live in slavery, or places of extreme heat or
     cold?
Or in pockets of poverty and fear
With areas of affluence all around them?
And others with freedom and plenty?

47

What about the children and parents,
Or women and men, that suffer abuse?
Should they be comforted
By being told that evil wil someday cease to exist?
What about the unborn who die—naturally or by
   abortion?
Or those whose lives are limited by physical affliction?

What is this individual life each of us has
With varying degrees of competence and awareness?

What I have shown you is that I join with the victim.

Just as the ground absorbs the blood you spill,
I absorb the pain and suffering you all
Inflict on others.

That really doesn't lessen the pain and suffering.
I can only assure you that it will end,
And that the righteous will live on.
And the evil and wicked will be cast out.

Will you have faith?
Will you trust me and perserve in following my ways?

VI
LOOKING AT THE WORLD

As we go through life, the going gets tough. We ask, why are things the way they are? We look for direction and signposts along the way. If we're committed to God, focused on God, the strength is somehow there to pass through the times of trial.

16. Commitment to Throw-away

We have created,
Lord,
A society that can discard.
Anything.
Everything.

We throw away the many things we grow tired of.
We throw away the old to get the new.
We try to throw away the difficult and get the easy.
We try to throw away that which is slow and get that
    which is quick.
And we want to make the old disappear quickly and
    quietly,
Without any fuss or bother.

We have commitment, Lord,
Toward that which is new and better, easier and faster.
We are making things more convenient.
We are committed to moving ahead.

Yes, my children,
You have made considerable progress
In learning how to make so much in your world.

But you need to look back
And see what is in your wake.
Your commitment to what you call progress
Is a dangerous commitment, because it lacks a
    responsibility
To care about the results of what you leave behind.
And it is dangerous because it lacks a responsibility
To care for and about people—your neighbors—
And people should come first.

In your rush for the quick and convenient

You put your throw-aways at the curb
Or in the woods
Or in the water
Or in the air
And forget about them.
Out of sight, out of mind?

I think you are learning now that
Delaying responsibility creates a worse problem
That has to be dealt with anyway,
Sooner or later.
But you have not learned about your responsibility to
    people.
You want to throw away people, too:
When they grow old
Or slow.
When they don't fit smoothly into your machines of
    production
You want to quickly and quietly replace them.

Stop for a moment
And look at all the instances where you make it
    happen:
Husbands and Wives, Parents and Children,
Old and Young, Majorities and Minorities,
Sick and Well, Ablebodied and Disabled,
Wealthy and Poor, Well-educated and Poorly-educated,
Employed and Unemployed.

You say that you want love and then fail to love.
You look for security and then destroy the security of
    others.
You argue you want peace and yet you make war.
You claim to want cleanliness but then pollute your
    own living space.

51

You want to be trusted and laugh at others who ask for
   your trust.
You seek tolerance for yourself and are intolerant of
   others.
You win by causing others to lose.
You want to receive
And to keep as well.

A commitment to this direction is only able to produce
   suffering
And death.
Can you see that this commitment to throw-away is
   going too far?

17. Mercy and Mystery

As often as I said, 'My foot has slipped,' your love, O
Lord, upheld me.
(*P 94:18*)

I am sometimes discouraged, Lord, and disillusioned
about the world, crying, as the psalmist does, "How long
shall the wicked triumph? They bluster in their insol-
ence." (*Ps 94:3,4*)

But, continuing on, I read, "As often as I said, 'My foot
has slipped,' your love, O Lord, upheld me." (*PS 94:18.*)

A thought dimly appears in my mind when I read this,
   Lord.
I seem to see in its vague light that we must come to
   you individually,
Acknowledging and lamenting our own slips.
And then, O Lord, you uphold us.

It is hard to understand and accept this, Lord.
We cry about the cruelty and violence of the wicked in
   the world.

You seem to ignore this
And simply tell us who pray that we should come to
   you.
In humble repentance,
For strength to live and not despair.

And we do. And we go on.
The world and its many peoples go on, too.

We, who want to be Christian, are in the midst of it
And yet must be apart from it.
We must participate in it and yet transcend it.
We must live in it and die in it. . .
Yet can choose to rise from it.

I think of the victims of wickedness.
I think of the victims of negligence.
I think of the victims of accidents and of nature.

I cry about the world as Job did. . .
As the psalmists did. . .
And you ask questions about our knowledge of your
   creation.

We are left only to fall down at your feet
And cry, Lord, have mercy on us.
And you do.

VII
FREEDOM AND OPPORTUNITY

God's admonition to love neighbor and self shows up constantly as we mature. We find that our individual Self is interdependent with that of others. The commandment, therefore, is in our own self-interest as well as the interest of our neighbor.

18. The Two Faces of Freedom

"If you abide in My word, then you are truly disciples of mine; and you shall know the truth, and the truth shall make you free."
(*Jn 8:31-32*)

Truth and Freedom, Lord,
Are things we claim to treasure;
Even though we often are not truthful—
With others, with you,
And even with ourselves.

We talk of being free.
Yet I see some awful behavior that people,
In their freedom,
Demonstrate to others,
And how this hurts and enslaves us.
How can you say we are free?

There are, my child, two ways of looking at freedom.
You are seeing only one of them.
One is illusion, seeking freedom from making
    decisions.
Here, even a slave is free.
Slaves are freed from making choices.
Choices are made for them.
They are coerced by a master to obey.

The other side is the real freedom.
This is the freedom to be free. . .to be alive. . .to be at
    peace.
But this freedom is harder to achieve—
For even while you constantly strive for it
The evil one works to drive you away from it
By deceiving you about freedom and leading you into
    slavery.

Real freedom must be bought with your life in truth.
Nothing more and nothing less.

But the price is worth it.

Truth is the path to freedom.
Truth is the way of life.

I am the way and the truth, and the life.
(*Jn 14:6*)
If you abide in My word, then you are truly disciples of
   mine;
And you shall know the truth, and the truth shall
   make you free.
(*Jn 8:31-32*)
This is my wish for you. Do you want it, too?

19. Be Peacemakers

Do you think I have come to give peace on earth?
(*Lk 12:51a*)
Strive for peace with all men, and for holiness without
which no one will see the Lord.
(*Heb 12:14*)

Grant us peace!

That is what many ask of me.
That is what many expect of me.
And when it doesn't come
You think I don't care
Or I don't exist
Or I just said no.

The problem is that
You aren't listening!

You want to interpret peace
As expecting not to be bothered by people or things.

And you seem to think it should happen automatically.
That's not what I said.
What I said was:
Strive for peace
With all people.

In other words,
You must be peacemakers!
Not peacetakers.

I have given you freedom,
Which means that you must labor to create a world
Free
From all that is not loving
And kind
And patient.

To do this, you have to be active.
You must be producers of peace,
Not passive takers.
And when you do this
You will truly learn
How it is in giving
That you receive.

I know that this is not easy
And that you will stumble along the way.
Please believe me when I say that you are not alone.
No matter how hard the going gets, I am with you.

20. Living Up to Your Potential

But to all who received him, who believed in his name,
he gave power to become children of God.
(*Jn 1:12*)

All who are led by the Spirit of God are sons of God. For
you did not receive the spirit of slavery, to fall back into

fear, but you received the spirit of sonship.
(*Rom 8:14,15*)

Not everyone who says to me Lord, Lord, shall enter the kingdom of heaven, but he who does the will of my father who is in heaven.
(*Mt 7:21*)

Lord,
In sports,
In school,
At work, or
At play,
We are encouraged to develop our potential.
We are asked to become all that we are capable of
    becoming.
And there is much to help us.

Yet all of this striving,
All this life-long effort
Is for the material things of some few years,
Sixty or seventy
Give or take.
And we leave it all behind.

Lord, what is the potential that you want us to
    develop?
If you came back today
What would you say
About Christians?
About me?

What I would say to you is this:
Love is your potential.
You are loved.
Love in return.

Can you see that if you don't,

Like it or not
You have chosen evil?

What, then, would we say to you, Lord?

Would we say, when did we see you hungry or thirsty,
A stranger, naked, sick or in prison,
And did not minister to you?
(*Mt 25:44*)

There seems to be so much holding back.
Even in the churches.
Clergy and laity are saying
I'm too busy. . .I don't know. . .I have to think about
    it. . .
I don't want to talk about it. . .It's personal. . .I don't
    have time. . .
I can't afford it . . . I don't agree.

How, Lord, do we know what to do?
Or when?
Where do we get the time and strength to realize our
    potential?

What I say to you is this:
By questioning, you have begun.

Do you love me?
Feed my sheep.

Seek to discover your talents
And use them in the service of others,
As opportunity allows.

Do you love me?
Feed my lambs.

Gather, as the Church.
I am the vine.
You are the branches.

60

Do you love me?
Will you take sustenance from me,
Helping one another
To understand and nurture your individual talents?

Will you develop your potential,
Become mature,
Bear fruit, and
Feed my sheep?

PART THREE

Building Greater
Awareness and Maturity

Eastern religions have people look within to discover that they are one with nature and having become aware of this to go into the world with a different perspective. Christians are taught to listen to that still small voice within, to test that voice with the teachings of the Bible so as to recognize and practice that which is good. Christians are told to love God, neighbor and self.

As we increase our awareness of God and ourselves, we begin to see more about the various peoples and groups we have to deal with, and question how to interact with them.

Preface
The Heart

CONSIDER THE HEART

IT IS A SYMBOL OF LOVE

IT RECEIVES LIFE'S BLOOD

IT GIVES LIFE'S BLOOD

WHEN IT STOPS GIVING

IT DIES

VIII
SEEING THE NEED FOR A SENSE OF COOPERATION

Cooperation does not seem to come naturally. We all like to advocate it when we want others to cooperate with us. But when it comes to doing what someone else needs, we are often reluctant or less than cheerful about it. The painful truth is that selfishness, not cooperating with what is right and good, is immature behavior. The "cure" is maturing. The beginning is to recognize that we all need to become more mature.

21. Of Birthrights and Human Nature

Many centuries ago a famous birth of twins occurred
And their lives are recorded in the Bible.
(*Gn 25:21-36:8*)
Esau was the firstborn
And thus the holder of the birthright,
The right to his father's inheritance and blessing.

Of this birth, it was foretold
That one shall be stronger than the other
And that the older shall serve the younger.
(*Gn 25:23-25*)

"Thus the last shall be first, and the first last."
(*Mt 20:16*)

Esau was known as a man of the field,
A skillful hunter.
His brother, Jacob, was known as a peaceful man,
Living in tents.

Esau, the hunter, enjoyed his freedom to roam.
He enjoyed the going out and the coming in.
One day he came in empty-handed, tired and hungry.
He wanted his brother to give him food.

Jacob offered him food
For the price of his twin brother's birthright!
A birthright that meant less than a meal:
As Esau said to Jacob, "I am about to die;
Of what use is a birthright to me?"
(*Gn 25:32*)

Jacob was a peaceful man
Who strove for his father's inheritance and blessing.
He supplanted his brother at a time when he was weak.
He gained his father's blessing at a time when he was
   weak.

He listened to his human impulses, as well as his
  mother's,
Even as Adam followed Eve.

Jacob lived on, with sufferings and joys, and became
  Israel.
Esau, too, went on to become a strong nation.
Both followed their human nature
And became strong, powerful and wealthy.
One knew God.
The other didn't see the need.

Jesus calls all people his brothers and sisters.
And he has food to give them.

And he offers if for free.
He gives people food for their physical hunger
And for their spiritual hunger.
(*Jn 6*)

Jesus said,
"It is the Spirit who gives life; the flesh profits nothing;
The words I have spoken are spirit and are life.
But there are some of you who do not believe."
(*Jn 6:63-64*)

Just as Esau and Jacob parted company
Many of Jesus' followers parted from him,
As his statements were such that they would not be-
  lieve,
Even though they knew his miracles.

Jesus turned to Peter and asked if he wanted to go, too.
Peter looked at Jesus and said,
"Lord, to whom shall we go? You have words of eternal
  life"
(*Jn 6:68*)

We are human,
And must live among people.
We are spiritual, too.

This spiritual nature is to do good and reject evil.
We are to be good, as God is good.
(*Mt 5:48*)

We do this by following Jesus
As he leads us to God.
He gives the Spirit of goodness
To empower us onward.

We are to resist a growing evil,
A progressive moving away from God.

Jesus shows us that the power of evil is so great
That he, while on the cross,
Was tempted by the pain to turn away from God,
Asking, "Why have you forsaken me?"

Thank God, he didn't turn away;
And thus is our light and our savior.

This is our birthright:
To grow in our humanity;
To grow in our spirituality;
To love, to move progressively closer to God;
And to accept our inheritance in the Kingdom of God.
Is your birthright something you are willing to give up?

22. Do We "No" the Wrong Things?

Lord, I feel down today.
A church leader has been telephoning people
To watch children in the nursery
For three Sundays during the year.
For nearly an hour, mother after mother says no.

Another committee asks for a pledge increase.
Most parishioners say no, even though they are no-
    where near tithing.

Another group has trouble getting people to set up for a
    function—
The non-employed are expected to do it all,
Because they have more time in a day than "working"
    people.

Another committee debates how many penitential ser-
    vices to hold before Easter
And whether to agree to a children's service at Christ-
    mas;
Too many services are tiring on the clergy.
The children's need for a service has to be argued.

A prayer group is formed and few come.
A Bible study is started and most stay away.
Lenten services are held and few attend.
Seminars are held on Christian family and few are
    there.

I wonder, Lord,
If there is so much reluctance within the Church,
How can things get better out there in society?

I guess this is not unusual, Lord,
But I have to ask you why?
Over the centuries you've given us prophets and signs
    to show the way.
Yet your people repeatedly turned away.
Abraham, Isaac and Jacob developed a community of
    free people.
They didn't hold fast and were enslaved.

Isaiah told them they were to be God's witnesses,
To show others that there is a God who loves all people

And who is willing and able to preserve their lives.
(*Is 43:10-13*)
Jeremiah told them to seek after the welfare of the
  community
To which they were carried off.
Not for punishment
But because their welfare depended on the city's wel-
  fare.
(*Jer. 29:7*)

Jesus came to show us your hope and love for us.
(*Jn 3:16*)
Most people still said no!
They saw the love.
The response was to reject and destroy him.
And yet, after people inflicted the most horrible tor-
  ture,
Jesus came back from this human made death,
Not in vengeance,
But in gentle humility,
Hands open to show his wounds,
Offering forgiveness,
And still more help to know and to live the truth.

You proved that the works of Godless people lead to
  suffering,
Destruction and death,
And that your works lead to love, joy and life.

Peter says we are ordained by you into a royal priest-
  hood,
A priesthood of all believers.
(*1 Peter 2:9*)
Isn't this real empowerment?
Didn't we take upon ourselves real vows
To you and humanity in Baptism,

And in Confirmation reaffirm these promises?

Yet all too often we sccm locked in our selfishness,
Seeking to protect our time and money.
But for what?
Time is spent, not saved.
What we spend on ourselves is withheld from others.
Don't we need a better balance, Lord?
Aren't we supposed to love you, and our neighbor, as
ourselves?

Aren't we all supposed to have enough time
And the right gifts from you to do all the work you
want?
It seems to me that when I try, it is not a burden.
It is not a chore.
It is a joyful experience.

But it is hard when so many don't want to help
In such important things.

Lord, are we a people who no the wrong things?

IX
LOOKING AT OURSELVES

Struggling again. Life is a constant struggle. Some people seem to have an easier go at it than others but we all experience difficulties. As we struggle with our lives, we find help from our faith in God.

23. The Irony of Price

Everything has a price.
We all know that.
And we all accept this fact,
Hoping to be able to buy the things we want—
Necessities and luxuries.

Then Jesus comes along and confuses us.
He accepts that things have a price and he pays it,
And encourages his disciples to purchase what is required for living.
But he also says not to worry about it too much.

Jesus tells us that life—everlasting life—is a gift of God.
It is free.
All we have to do is follow him and obey God's laws.

But isn't that a price?
A very high price?

Isn't that giving up our freedom?
Doesn't that limit our choices?
Limit what we want to do?

"Take up your cross," he says.
Isn't that an awfully high price?
Who can walk into all that pain and suffering?
That's a price that so very few can pay!

A price, my children, is what you pay for the work of another.
There is no price that you can pay me for my work.

What could you pay me for your life? Money? Gold? Jewels?
All these are mine already.
The universe is mine.

Your life is what is valuable.
It is something I have already bought.

The price was my incarnation,
My very own life.
I give it to you. All you have to do is accept it as a gift.
To accept life what you need to do is love.

You deceive yourself by looking for happiness any-
    where else.
All else is self-deception.
All else leads to pain and suffering.
That is the price you pay.

When you look at someone who loves,
You may think they pay a high price of losing their own
    self.
But when you, yourself, become the lover,
You will find the idea of price to be an illusion.
By loving, you remove the price.

Let those who are thirsty come.
Let those who desire
Take the water of life without price.
(*Rev 22:17*)

See if my words are not true.
Learn about love.
Practice doing it.

Then ask yourself,
Is this not refreshment without price?

24. Alone is Empty

I and me,
I gotta be me!
And you gotta be you.

So in this life
We organize to compete.
Rugged individuals we become
In order to blossom and flourish.

Individuals with life;
Alone yet among others.
We succeed or fail alone;
Feeling joy and pain alone.

Some seek to rule,
Finding neither happiness nor safety
In their power over people and things.

Lord, what I seem to feel, in all this, is that
Individually, I have life but life individually is empti-
    ness.
Yet in the midst of all this striving I hear that
It is in sharing life with others that I can find peace.
It is in cooperating with you and my neighbors,
And having them cooperate with me,
That we all achieve a more lasting and secure state of
    well-being.

But we pay such lip-service to this idea,
This need for cooperation.
Why?

Every good structure starts with a good foundation.
In life, it is the relationship between me and you.
Jesus told you that the first Commandment
Was to love the Lord your God with all your heart,
With all your soul, with all your mind and with all your
    strength.
And that the second
Was to love your neighbor as yourself.
(*Mk 12:30-31*)

78

You cannot do the second without the first.
If you try you are attempting to make yourself to be
   God
And it is impossible for you to do that.

I love you. When you love me in return,
And then try to love your neighbor as yourself,
You will find,
To your very great surprise and happiness,
That your aloneness disappears,
Your individuality flourishes,
And your emptiness and longing for fulfillment is gone.

I long for that time.
Do you long for it too?
Will you find your life by giving it to me
That I may give it back to you?

25. Pride and Humility

There is a story told of how a woman—not an Israel-
ite—approached Jesus, asking him to heal her daugh-
ter. Jesus ignored her. She kept after him and his disciples asked Jesus to send her away. Jesus tried to do
this by telling her that he was sent only to the lost
sheep of Israel.

The woman persisted and Jesus refused her again saying, rather harshly, that it wouldn't be fair for him to
take the children's bread and throw it to the dogs. The
woman then responded that even the dogs manage to
eat the crumbs that fall from their masters' tables.
(Mt 15:22-28)

Many times I have read this story, Lord.
It is always beautiful
And moving.

I listen to the woman
Pleading with you.
I hear you protesting—
Seeming to display a prejudice—
That since she wasn't from the House of Israel
You needn't be concerned about her needs.
I can see your humanness.
We all tend to take care of our own first.

But quickly the scene changes
And the woman's brilliant, creative argument
Wins you over
And you grant her desire.

We now can see that
Anyone can come to you and be healed.

But I am secretly envious about the brilliance
Of the woman's argument
That led you to turn
From a harsh refusal to help.

Would I,
In such a circumstance,
Be bright enough and clever enough
To make such a good argument
That you would change your mind and help me?

Or would I just be dejected
And slowly walk away,
Embarrassed and helpless,
Because I was not smart enough
To win you over?

Or angry,
And just go about life without you?

80

I see that you do not understand
The story
Or the woman.

Her response
Was not a brilliant argument,
Even if it appears that way.

A brilliant argument
Comes from the intellect—
A mind working with clever pride
Trying to win a victory,
Striving to make a sale.

Her response
Was from the heart,
In humility.

It was her humility
Her lack of pride,
That allowed her to see
Her need of me
And that my love
Would not be withheld
From her.

Can you see?
A sense of humility is not weakness.
It is great power.

PART FOUR

Growing Toward Cooperation with God

As we continue on the road toward maturity, we find ourselves being concerned with two realms. One is spiritual, with questioning about spirituality maturity. The other, earthly, is about community, asking questions about leadership in the world, and seeking the wisdom and knowledge to know and to do God's will.

Preface
The Good Life: A
Necessary Balance

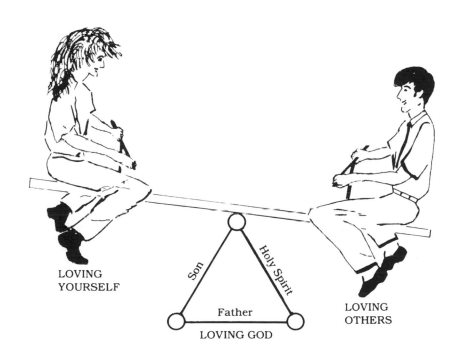

LOVING
YOURSELF

Son

Holy Spirit

Father

LOVING GOD

LOVING
OTHERS

85

X
SEEING SPIRITUALITY

Adulthood is a process of evolving a mature outlook on life and accepting our part in caring about the world and the people in it. This is an intelligent caring that comes from knowledge and wisdom, balanced with love and guidance from God.

26. Our Spiritual Nature

Jesus spoke of a tiny mustard seed,
Comparing it to faith;
It is so small
Yet it develops into something big.

A man and a woman come together,
Attracted by love.
They join and their seed,
So tiny as to be unseen with the eye,
Unite and a new life is begun!

This life is a fulfilling of two people
Who have joined together
In a freely giving, loving union.
In a sense, it is eternal life;
A vital part of each partner fuses
To form a new human being
With traits—an essence—transferred from each parent.

The importance of this creation
Is recognized deep within us.

In our humanity we are to each other
Husband or wife,
And to another, neighbor;
And as we grow in life
We also nurture our children
And teach them how to grow.

In our family,
We learn to live a sense of community,
Extended to become society
And further extended to be civilization.
This is the nature of our humanity.

We are also designed by God

To go beyond our humanity,
To transcend our human nature.

The Alpha—the beginning, Christ—
Has offered us eternal life:
Offered to our ancestors, ourselves,
And our children;
And we are all in a sense one,
Even one with him,
If we just choose to be with him:
The Omega—the end, Christ—
Will unite us with him, with God.

We are affected by good and evil,
Truth and lies, life and death.
And as a result we act!
And that action can be toward truth and good and
    life—
Toward that which we call God;
Or that action can be toward sin: lies, evil, and death.

Our human nature is a worldly nature.
No matter how hard we try to be young and healthy
    and attractive,
We are all on a march toward earthly death.
So, we have to learn to live our earthly life well
Even while learning to live our spiritual life.

Our spiritual nature is of God.
It is a nature of truth, for it is reality.
It is a nature of good, for it is love.
It is a nature of life, for it is God.

Sadly, we can live a life of denials:
Of our humanity by the way we treat ourselves and
    others;
Of our spirituality by denying God
And our own eternity.

Lord, why do we seem to have so much of a problem
Understanding and accepting our spiritual nature?

Why do we not take our spiritual nature,
Which operates on our conscious and unconscious
  minds
And helps us to live a better and happier life,
  seriously enough?

Is our faith too small?

The size of your faith is not important.
What is important is where you are planted,
Where your roots are.
Even as the tiny mustard seed germinates into some-
  thing big,
Even as your seed produces human life,
You will live and grow properly if you are sown in me.

27. The Helper

The wind blows where it wishes and you hear the sound
of it, but do not know where it comes from and where it
is going; so is everyone who is born of the spirit.
(*Jn 3:8*)

He will teach you all things, and bring to your remembr-
ance all that I have said to you.
(*Jn 14:26*)

This is kind of difficult to buy, Lord.
You're telling me that you are sending a helper
But I won't know where it comes from or where it is
  taking me?
And I will not be able to see it or hear it?
I will just "remember" things you want me to know?
And then I'm supposed to do it?
Right?

90

How do I know it's you, God?
Couldn't you be a little more direct?
There are some strange people going around doing
    strange things,
Or even horrible things,
Saying you told them to do it.
I don't want to be like that!

Every teacher or parent knows it is easier to do some-
    thing yourself
Than to help other people learn how, and do it them-
    selves.
And you can also go around ordering people to do
    things.
But that develops a dependent and coercive atmo-
    sphere.

What I am about is teaching you how to live—
With yourself, your neighbor, and with me.
I know that there are evil deeds
That are reputed to have been inspired by me.
But that is false.
Good people will not be misled
Because from me only truth and goodness come.
You should test every thought and deed you feel you
    want to do.
If it has been brought by the Spirit, it will be right and
    good.

As you continue in this process,
you will grow in communion with me.
Sharing in a life that is good.

Through this process you will gain independence,
For you will be entirely trustworthy.
You will be truly free, with a perfect freedom

That includes and encompasses all that is right and
  joyful.

Your growth,
Your will to choose what is good is most important to
  me.
That is why I offer so much help.
I know it can be hard to hear,
But if you want to hear, you will hear.
I know it can be hard to follow
But if you want to follow, you will be able to follow.
Not as a slave.
As a free person.

You will be alive
In a universe so vast and beautiful
As to be unimaginable to your mind.
It will take eternity to live and love it.

I have put it in writing.
The Spirit and the Bride say Come!
(*Rev 22:17*)

What will you do?
If you don't come, where are you going?

28. Like Breathing In and Breathing Out

Love and God.
Like breathing in and breathing out.

We breathe in God
By the help of Jesus.

And in accepting his life and teaching
About our God
And about life
We breathe out love.

And in the breathing in
And in the breathing out
We live.
And it is good.

But if in the breathing in we breathe not God,
And if in the breathing out we breathe not love,
There is no life.
For it is the breathing in of God
that gives us the power to love.

It is in the loving that we live.

Breathe in God.
Let God fill your lungs
And your blood
And feed your body and mind
With all the nourishment you need to live.
You will gain knowledge and wisdom and strength.

Then when you breathe out
You will breathe out love.
And there will be joy!

Not all at once;
And not all the time,
In the here and now.
We must persist.

Love and God.
Like breathing in and breathing out.

29. Wellness

Where there not ten cleansed? But the nine—where are
they? Was no one found who turned back to give glory
to God except this foreigner? And he said to him, Rise
and go your way; your faith has made you well.
(*Lk 17:17-19*)

Lord, I heard this story in church today.
It was familiar.
My mind raced through it before the reader finished
    the first sentence.

Yet something has always bothered me.
You tell the Samaritan his faith made him well.
But you already cured him!
And the other nine, too!

I was thinking about that
And was startled with another understanding.
You weren't speaking only of his physical wellness.

This is similar to another story,
The one where you pronounced forgiveness of a crip-
    pled man's sins
And when the religious leaders grumbled that only
    God, not you,
Can forgive sins,

You asked if it was easier to heal a cripple than forgive
    sins.
And then healed the cripple.

All this time I have not seen that the healing the faith
    produced
Was an inner wellness we get by recognizing and ac-
    cepting you.

The lesson is not that nine out of ten healed were too
    busy
Or careless to thank you, but to show us that real well-
    ness
Comes by our recognition of who you are and what we
    are,
And our coming to you.

94

This act of our will demonstrates our faith.
And you confirm that it is faith that makes us well.

We can come to you on our feet, on our knees, or flat
    on our back.
It doesn't matter.
You are there to welcome and accept us.
You are there to proclaim our sins forgiven.
You are there to tell us to rise and go, our faith has
    made us well-
If not in body
In spirit,
Which is where our life really is.

Can it be that nine out of ten of us
Live at the material surface of life,
And never stop to consider the depths
Of ourselves
And come to have faith
Through your love of us
And our feeble but adequate attempts
To love you in return?

What is it about us, Lord,
That makes us think that we can be well
Without you?

XI

DEVELOPING A SENSE OF COMMUNITY

In this group we begin to assess the idea of rights and responsibilities. We have spiritual rights and responsibilities. We have political rights and responsibilities too, as Jesus indicated in his response about paying taxes, when he told us to render unto Caesar what is Caesar's.

30. A Wise Investment in Real Estate

It is said

That those who are wise

Invest in

Real Estate

"Real"—True and Actual

"Estate"—A Condition of Life, Wealth or Status

The best real estate deal around

Is the one offered you by God!

Isn't that what you ought to invest in?

(For more information, read God's prospectus—the Bible!)

31. Rivalry—Chasing Winds

And I have seen that every labor and every skill which is done is the result of rivalry between a man and his neighbor. This too is vanity and striving after wind.
(*Eccl 4:4*)
Come to Me, all who are weary and heavy-laden, and I will give you rest.
(*Mt 11:28*)

Lord Jesus,
You invite
ALL,
Not just the bright and pretty and young,
As we tend to do,
To come to you
For your help and your peace.

We create so much pressure
On ourselves, our children,

98

Our neighbors.

Everything is rivalry!
It is so today, as it was nearly 2,400 years ago
When Ecclesiastes was written.

You seek cooperation. We seek competition.
You seek compassion. We seek winning.
But what do we get from following our way?

Many get high. . .
On drugs or alcohol. . .
On violence—we are even entertained by mayhem. . .
On money—
On sex.

Yet we are increasingly unhappy,
Sometimes causing others to be broken and unhappy
    too.

Our solution, it seems,
Is to follow a path of violence and abuse to ourselves,
To you and to our neighbors.

All is rivalry and striving after wind.
Even when we win what we seek, the satisfaction is
    only momentary.
Our peace is fleeting.
There is no rest.
We seem driven on to the next chase.

We do not learn that there is no real victory possible in
    this quest.
We seem unable to trust
your promise of life and your help to get us there.

You call.
We do not answer.
We are afraid.

We grasp tenaciously to this life we can hold in our
    hands
Even for a little while.

Lord, Jesus Christ, you came to show us the way;
Continue to have mercy on us,
As we struggle to know and to do your will.

32. An Incurious People

The government. . .
The state. . .

We are fascinated by these human creations.
Some view them almost as parents, there to take care
    of our needs,
While we go out to play.

We obey them and rebel against them.
We are led, even coerced,
Into conforming to the collective thinking
Of these power structures,
Whose operators seek—and are asked—
To do more and more for people;
Growing bigger and bigger
And taking more and more control;
Becoming less and less responsive to people,
As it grows larger and more powerful.

Is it not true that what is important is all individuals?
Then why is it that a bigger state,
Grown to serve us more,
Takes away so much from us
And leaves so many with less?

The structure that your predecessors created is good.
Your government, in your own words,
Is of the people, by the people and for the people.

You say you are one nation, under God, with liberty
    and justice for all.
This is good.

The problem is that so many have ceased to mature.
You are thus paying only lip-service
To the worth and dignity of the individual,
Because that worth increases from becoming mature
    people,
Accepting responsibilities for yourself and each other.

You must constantly work to become mature,
Because immaturity makes life
In this complex world
More painful for you. . .
For your children. . .
And their children. . . .

All of these thoughts and ideas are not new.
They have been there for thousands of years.
I've even had it all written down for you.
It's the best self-help book ever published.
It shows you what to do and how to do it.
Do you read the Bible?

It really is a matter of life and death.
Believe it!

33. Give Strength to Others

Simon, Simon, behold, Satan has demanded permis-
sion to sift you like wheat; but I have prayed for you,
that your faith may not fail; and you, when once you
have turned again, strengthen your brothers.
(*Lk 22:31-32*)

Lord, your prayer and charge is powerful in its love

And awesome in its message to us.
In it I feel so many emotions.

I feel a sense of fear and anxiety about being sifted.
I feel a concern about facing a difficult
And perhaps painful experience.

Your words give me a sense of the pain that you bear,
Like my sending my child into a hospital operating
    room:
He goes, trusting in me. I let him go, in trust.
We are both apprehensive.
We both hope for a better life in the future.

I sense a tenderness in you, too,
And feel your heart reaching out to Peter.
I feel that in this act something incredible happened:
Humble and powerful in your love and hope,
You passed your mantle on—
To Peter—
Making him the rock upon which to build your Church.

And it is for us too: your prayer gives us power to sur-
    vive,
Yet we must do more than that.
After passing through the ordeal
We must use our new strength to strengthen others.

I will help you to see what is good and what is right.

Will you try to strengthen your brothers and sisters
And neighbors
Whenever you have the opportunity?

CONCLUSION
Understanding Leadership And Community

Jesus was constantly going out into the communities, teaching, healing, helping. He also sent his disciples out into the world. Their life was one of going out and coming back to him and going out again. We find that as we come closer to God and let ourselves be sent out to work in the world, in concert with God, that this work, while difficult and challenging, is something that is fulfilling.

34. A Dream About Leaders

I have a dream about the Church and Christianity.
In the dream there's a vision of leadership in the world
Where many Christians can become leaders—
At home, at work, at play, at church;
In local communities, national events, and foreign af-
    fairs;
With things that are humble as well as great.

It's a vision which perceives
That those who truly know and follow God
Are able to be real leaders in the world.
For true Leaders are people with vision
To see what is needed and what is right;
Who can mobilize other people
And all the resources necessary
To get those right things done.

Sometimes these leaders may be known only to God,
For they can work in the background—
Even performing a simple act of kindness;
Their seeing a right need and fulfilling it
Going unrecognized for the real leadership it is.

It is a dream where people look to Jesus
And not only call him Lord
But go out into cities and towns
As doers of what is needed
And what is right.

Churches, in this dream,
Are places where Christians
Are nurtured, comforted, strengthened and empow-
    ered,
To go forth into the world as Christ did,
Knowing they will use many of his words as they go:

104

be done" . . .
: the flesh is weak" . . .
/es" . . .

)rsaken me?"

t cross and follow you.
)? You have the Words of Life.

ayer
ll be able to say

ommend my spirit.